MW00977800

See the Good in You

Finding clarity for your personal brand

See the Good in You

Finding clarity for your personal brand

Jen Campbell

Red Lips Marketing, McCall, Idaho

Copyright © 2020 Jen Campbell

All rights reserved. No portion of this book may be reproduced in any form without express permission in writing from the publisher.

ISBN: 978-1-7359955-0-2

Dedication

To the 12-year-old Jen who wanted to be a writer.
And to everyone who has supported her dream since then.
Thank you.

Table of Contents

Dedication 5

Table of Contents 7

What's personal branding?..8

Your box of stuff 10

The freedom in being fired 16

Transition Times 19

Public Shaming..22

How do you want to be remembered?................................28

Listening to your inner voice 32

Who we were 36

When you thought you could 40

Our labels 45

The foundation of our support system 50

How I fixed the dresser I should have said no to 53

The Scream 56

5 tips for setting goals 59

Day one..63

Our Perception 65

A note from the author..71

FAQs 72

What's personal branding?

Personal branding is who you are, and how you present that to the world in a manner which allows others to see the good in you, and what you do.

I'm Jen Campbell, Personal Branding Expert and Entrepreneurial Connector. I help people gain clarity to expand their community, connections, and conversions through strategy, coaching and mentorship.

A few years ago, I worked to define my personal brand. I evaluated the stories of my past, and I dug into all the things in "my box of stuff" both physically and mentally. As part of that process, I wrote a blog. I've adapted several of the stories I shared on my blog for this book.

I spent most of my life limited by labels imposed on me both by others and myself. The process I used to define myself, and the core characteristics of my personal brand, is the foundation of this workbook. The reflective questions are part of the process that I use with my clients to help them hone and refine their personal brand. I teach my clients to position themselves in the marketplace by showing the best versions of themselves.

This is a book of self-discovery.

I'm a storyteller, and have learned that the stories we tell ourselves are the most important stories. They also impact the authenticity with which we can share our personal brand with others in a way that feels good.

Typically, my life transition times have been the biggest opportunity for me to reflect, reposition and grow. Personally, it seems to occur in a 5 year cycle with massive changes in my life. 2020 has allowed a valuable opportunity for growth with a lot of transition times. It has been a valuable opportunity to reflect, rejuvenate and refine my personal brand and purpose.

You don't need to do every exercise in the book. There is no test, or grade at the end. Choose at least one thing you discover through this process, and act upon it, so you can grow. I believe that understanding who you are is the foundational principle of successful personal branding.

Dig deep and unpack some stuff you've been carrying with you for awhile now. It can be uncomfortable.

It will be worth it.

The goal is personal growth to be able to see the good in you and what you do.

Are you ready?

Let's do this!

PS As a thank you for purchasing this book, I have a special bonus for you:

https://RedLipsMarketing.com/bonus

Your box of stuff

The physical things we save are a reflection of who we are.

Most people have at least one. Others have a storage unit full of them. They're the Rubbermaid bins and cardboard boxes of memories. They are full of photographs, newspaper clippings, cards and mementos. It's what you've moved with you during your life's journey. It's what you've valued or what you want to be remembered for, or never want to forget. It's your personal history. It is your box of stuff.

Watching the movie Citizen Kane for the first time, at 14 years old, I cried when they tossed Charles Foster Kane's sled Rosebud in the fire. I cried because no one knew what was most important to a public figure... and that the world was so quick to judge him for tangible accomplishments rather than his intent. They didn't really know out of all the stuff he owned what he valued or why. Although he was able to amass a fortune, he never communicated that effectively as part of his personal brand.

On a vacation, I tracked a distant cousin down while visiting near her home in Texas. I asked to see the boxes of stuff left to her after her maternal grandmother died. She allowed me to spend hours in her office photographing what was in the boxes. *It was one of the best things that I did on my vacation.* She asked me, like so many others have, why I care so much about the lives of strangers. Why would I take the time to research, record and preserve records of people that I am not even related to?

By honoring our dead, and acknowledging their lives and contributions, we are connected. Their legacy is preserved and can serve as an example to others...

or a cautionary tale. By spending my time documenting the losses of spouses, children, jobs, and homes, I hope to preserve that legacy, and remind myself why I need to keep working towards becoming the person I want to be.

The importance of pushing through the pain and losses we all endure in life, are what define us... not the losses.

By preserving a person's legacy, we honor their strength, and can develop empathy for the magnitude of the burdens they carried in life.

My work as a family historian has guided me to see the good in people. That can be challenging when there is little information that I can piece together from a person's life. No photographs. No living relatives to talk to. No way to confirm what I can surmise about a person's character based on details I fit together to create a vision of who someone was, and what they did or did not accomplish in the time they spent on this earth.

After someone dies, sometimes, you will inherit a box of their stuff. After you lose someone, it may take time to open it, but please, keep it. Label the outside if you're not ready to immerse yourself in its contents. Someday, even if *you* never open it, there might be someone who cares, and wants to document the details from their life so that person's legacy is preserved.

Back to your box of stuff... When was the last time you opened it? Are there things you need to cull from its contents? What should you add? If that was all someone had to define you, what would they know about you and how you have changed throughout your life? If it doesn't reflect the essence of who you are, change it while you can. That is part of who you are, and the foundational part of your personal brand.

And if you are feeling really ambitious, please, *label those pictures*, and put a note explaining your stuff and why it's valuable. It may take time, and require introspection you usually avoid, but do it anyway. Your legacy will thank you.

Questions for reflection

Get your box of stuff... the one with the oldest stuff. There are reasons why you valued those items, and saved them.

Create a pile of items from your box which bring you joy. What do you notice about the joyful pile? How do those items reflect your accomplishments and strengths?

Write down at least 3 words that come to your mind when you look at your joyful pile.

What is left in the other pile from your box of stuff that doesn't bring you joy?

_____

_____

_____

_____

Is there a common theme to the items?
A painful point in your life it reminds you of? Is it a toxic person? A loved one who has died? Do you remember why you originally saved those things?

_____

_____

_____

What purpose do these items serve?

_____

_____

_____

Consider letting go of items that cause you pain, resentment, angst or other negative emotions. Or, tuck it back into your box until you're ready to deal with it. That's okay too.

Is there anything you need to add to your box of stuff that showcases the best parts of who you are, and important moments in your life?

_____

_____

_____

The freedom in being fired

The end of one thing ushers in the beginning of something new.

At 21, I was hired as a temp to work in the HR department for a company owned by Paul Allen, the co-founder of Microsoft, to assist with annual reviews. It involved filing, following up with emails and data entry. I hoped that the job would lead to a full time position with the company.

I had been working for three weeks when the head of HR and my direct supervisor called me into an office to fire me. They explained that the two of them had spent several hours correcting my errors. Both women were professional and polite, and told me how much they enjoyed me as a person, but this just wasn't the right job for me. They told me:

"Attention to detail is not one of your strengths."

It was the most important thing my supervisor told me when I was fired, because it was true, and nearly two decades later, it's still true.

It could be that I'm an ENFP according to the Myers Brigg personality test. It may be the ADD I was diagnosed with as an adult. Maybe, it's neurological mapping. The why doesn't really matter. Being fired from a prestigious job that I thought I wanted taught me more about what I needed in a career, and the type of environment where I would thrive.

Knowing that attention to detail isn't one of my strengths gave me the insight to turn down future data entry positions. It inspired me to hire a detail oriented team when I managed retail locations for Starbucks. (My store had the cleanest floor drains in town.) It gave me the courage to turn the bookkeeping for our small business over to an accountant, so I could focus on spending more time with my children. It also gave me the desire to search for the things that *are* my strengths and help them shine.

Questions for reflection

Have you ever been fired?

_____

_____

_____

How has being fired from a job or quitting one helped you?

_____

_____

_____

How are you spending the majority of your time now? How could you enjoy it more?

_____

_____

_____

Transition Times

Our reason for change

Our life transitions bring the valuable gift of time. It's time to reevaluate our priorities, and to reflect on and set new goals. Sometimes, transitions encourage us to change a life path we are on, and choose another. Its end as well as the beginning of something new.

I have four sons. The oldest three or triplets. My youngest son's October birthday missed the Kindergarten cutoff this year by about a month. Since June, I have fantasized about the time when all my children would be in school during the day, and I would be at home. I would have to finish home repairs, to craft, to write, to run and to have quiet during the day. I've longed for time to reconnect with myself, and spend time savoring solitude. He started preschool today, and I have cried a lot.

And I cried yesterday.

And the day before that.

And I finally figured out why something I've anticipated would cause such sadness. My son starting school signals a transition period in my life, and it's a reminder of my mortality.

Our life transitions bring the valuable gift of time.

It's time to reevaluate our priorities, and to reflect on and set new goals. Sometimes, transitions encourage us to change a life path we are on, and choose another. It's the end as well as the beginning of something new.

New can be exciting, but when you long for the comfort of the known, it can be overwhelming. As I transition to the role of a mother of school age boys, there are things that I miss. The greatest longing comes with knowing my role is different now. I don't have a baby to nurse in the middle of the night or someone to teach and guide through a year of first milestones. As my children age, and gain autonomy, I find myself losing a part of motherhood I've enjoyed more than I thought I would... nurturing.

During this life transition, I've spent time envisioning how my role as a mother will continue to shift over the next decade as my triplets age, mature, and move away from home. As my motherhood role transitions, I can use the opportunity to grow and change.

The best part of life transitions is that they give us the power to re-focus, show gratitude, and to savor the moments of our journey, however long or short it is. I believe it's the collection of life's transitions that help us learn the most and to reach our personal potential... even if we have to reach for the tissues often in the process.

Questions for reflection

What life transition time are you going through right now?

_____

_____

_____

How has that transition time motivated your desire to change?

_____

_____

_____

_____

_____

Public Shaming

How we treat others, reflects our character.

It was a picture of a lady's feet getting a pedicure next to my friend. The towel under her feet was littered with dead skin hunks that had been sloughed off her feet. It was pretty gross.

My friend had snapped a picture of this woman's feet, posted it to Facebook, and made a remark about all the dead skin. Within moments, there were several comments about the condition of this woman's feet and 1 share.

I contemplated adding to the comments, but didn't know what to say. I wanted the acceptance of a "like" on my comment from my friends. I didn't like the picture or comment, but it has bothered me a lot, and I finally figured out why.

Public Shaming.

Public shaming isn't anything new. People have been ridiculed for not fitting in, for being different, for not being "normal" (whatever that means) as long as people have been on Earth. We might not keep a person in the town square in stocks. We don't stone people in the public commons. We don't make women pin scarlet letters to their chests for adultery. Children are not relegated to the corner of the classrooms to wear dunce caps. But, we still publicly shame people.

Social media has created a platform to disseminate information rapidly, and has been increasingly used to shame, humiliate and degrade others, and often they aren't even people we know. Some people even post pictures of their pets with signs on social media platforms publicly shaming them for alleged misdeeds.

I have known this girl since high school. I remember her as kind, and that's why it surprised me so much. It seemed out of character for her to point out something negative about a stranger. She is a lot like me, and it made me question my behavior. As I thought about that woman's feet, throughout my day yesterday, my discomfort grew, because I became more aware. I started thinking about the rest of the woman these feet were attached to, and how much her feet were like mine.

Renowned psychiatrist, William Glasser focused a lot of his studies on our 5 basic needs. One of them is a sense of belonging, love and acceptance. We want to feel like we are part of something. We want to feel included, liked and admired. We want to fit in. Well, most of us do.

There are those that take pride in their differences, and stand out from the crowd based on their appearance, occupation, lifestyle, and how they spend their time. Most of those people still hang out with others who share their differences.... It's that whole birds of a feather flock together colloquialism my grandmother used.

Publicly shaming others can create a false sense of belonging, and acceptance with our peers. That's part of why we do it.

I can think of at least 10 movies about high school, its drama and social hierarchy without a search engine. The movies continue to resonate with past and present generations, because high school is a microcosm for the rest of your life. I didn't believe that during high school. Hope that life in "the real world" would be different or better is part of what helped me survive those four years. People want to fit in. They want to be included, and they will sometimes do things out of character to feel that sense of belonging.

Most of the popular people at my high school were athletes. We had several state champion teams in a variety of sports. Some of the popular athletes were kind, and others were masters of public shaming. There were usually one or 2 leaders of the group, and the others who would contribute to the humiliation or would condone it through their silence or lack of defense for the persecuted. We didn't have bullying rules when I was in high school, but I don't know if that would have made a difference.

Most of the time it wasn't a dramatic, direct attack on the individual like memorable scenes from high school movies. (I'm not aware of hazing that occurred.) It was more often sarcasm, and indirect ridicule. It was subtle whispers and gossip. It was painful. It was public shaming, and I had a problem with it twenty years ago too.

During high school, Maria* was known by many for being mean. She was smart, and had an ability to hone in on a person's vulnerabilities to shame them. I'd been on the receiving end of her remarks and experienced humiliation more than once. I had also defended several people she and her friends had attacked, both publicly and privately. I was glad when I didn't have to interact with her everyday. I saw her when she was at college once, in 1997, and she had changed. I was apprehensive about what she would say to me. I was guarded, and didn't understand why my high school friends would be associating with her in college, when they hadn't been close friends.

She hugged me.

She told me that I looked good. I was waiting for the but... or the cutting sarcasm, but it never came. What came instead, to my disbelief, was an apology for how she had treated me and so many other people. She told me that she admired that I stood up for people, and I was generally kind to everyone. I saw compassion and vulnerability in a person I thought lacked either one. That was the Maria my friends who went to college and high school with knew.

She was kind.

I am grateful it's my final memory of her. She died from a heart attack, due to an undiagnosed heart condition about 6 months later. I wish that more people were able to see who she had become, and her compassion. We don't always know our lasting impact on the lives of others - both positively and negatively.

I spent a couple of hours this morning physically preparing for an evening out. I gave myself a pedicure, and thought of the picture of the lady's feet. I rarely take time or spend money on "pampering myself".

What if the woman in my friend's picture is like me? Perhaps, she got a pedicure certificate for Mother's Day, she's finally getting to use it at the end of June. Or, looked at her feet, as she slipped them in her sandals, and saw how the hours she'd spent on them, working and tending to the needs of others had taken their toll. Maybe, she had to call 4 people before finding someone who could watch her kids for her to take time to care for herself. Maybe, she is preparing for an evening out, and wants to feel young and beautiful in high heeled peep-toe shoes she saves for special occasions that don't come very often.

Really, the reason why doesn't matter.

I don't think less of my friend for posting the picture. I still think that she is kind and compassionate.

It's not about a picture of a woman's feet. It is how we perceive the vulnerabilities in others, and what we do with those vulnerabilities.

We are all like Maria at both points in her life. Sometimes, we are leading the public shaming, and sometimes we realize that what we ridicule in others may be what we feel most vulnerable about.

May we all show more kindness, compassion and caring before we shame and judge. The truth is, it's not just the person who leads the attack on another person who is guilty. It is each of us who allow public shaming to continue through our actions or lack thereof .

name changed

Questions for reflection

When was the last time you were publicly shamed? (This could have been online or in person.)

_____

_____

_____

_____

What was it about?

_____

_____

How did it make you feel?

_____

_____

How do you want to be remembered?

The way we are remembered is a reflection of our lives, and the impression we leave on others.

People die. I know that the only way that I'll be able to avoid it is if I am still on the earth for the rapture. Fingers crossed. Since no one really knows when that's going to happen, there's not anyway to plan to avoid death.

When I was 13, I wanted to live to be 117 years old. It seemed like a reasonable number given longevity in my genetics and medical advancements. I figured that it was the only way I'd be able to accomplish everything that I want to do on this earth before I'm gone. I'm not sure that's what I want anymore.

The longer you live, you inevitably experience more pain and loss. While I know logically that the bitter helps me to appreciate the sweet, it doesn't take the sting or pain away from the loss or the crummy parts of life. Because, sometimes life is really hard.

It's painful.

It's discouraging.

Some days, you need to close your eyes to stop the tears. You need to put your hand on your heart to know that it's still beating and not broken.... even though it feels like it is.

There is a sweet lady named Dorothy that I attend church with. She's in her 90's. She's bright, and has a delightful sense of humor. When I envision life in my 90's, I think of her.

I complimented her on an intricately carved ivory necklace she was wearing one Sunday. Dorothy told me that her husband bought it and mailed it to her when he was serving overseas during World War II. She explained that he had died a long time ago, but she liked to wear the necklace to remember him.

Dorothy has endured the deaths of her husband, and most of her children. Yesterday, I realized that if I live to be 117, most of the people that I love will die before I do. This realization made me feel isolated.

I believe in life after death. I believe that part of what we can take with us, is our relationships, experiences and knowledge. That core belief motivates me to cultivate relationships, and learn and grow as much as possible while I'm alive.

Yesterday, I learned of the sudden death of a former high school classmate. It caused me to realize how many more funerals, memorial services and deaths that I will experience if I live to be 117 years old.

When a person leaves this earth, what legacy do they leave behind?

Some men have buildings dedicated to their memories, or a child that bears their name, or companies that they have built. They spend lifetimes building wealth or cultivating a legacy.

Most people are not extraordinary.

Their names aren't recorded in history books. They don't achieve great fame or wealth. They live and die, and are remembered only by relatives and friends.

When those relatives and friends die, how is a person's legacy preserved? How are they remembered and honored?

> *"Show me the manner in which a nation cares for its dead and I will measure with mathematical exactness the tender mercies of its people, their respect for the laws of the land and their loyalty to high ideals." -William Gladstone*

I hope to continue to cultivate new friendships as I age. The more connected I am to others, my hope is that I will leave a greater legacy through my shared experiences with others.

I long to develop greater resiliency despite the trials in my life, and the loved ones that I lose.

I want my life to be defined not by its length or way it ends, but how I've spent my collection of moments.

Questions for reflection

What words do you want people to use to describe you after you die?

_____

_____

_____

_____

What do you want them to remember about you?

_____

_____

_____

_____

Listening to your inner voice

Listen to your inner voice about how you want to reflect who you are physically, and be seen by others.

I put the aqua blue sequin tank dress on lay-away in February. I had satin aqua pumps and a purse dyed to match it. As I earned tips from my job as a Barista, I paid for it $20 at a time. Usually, my mom went with me to shop for formal dance dresses, but I was 17, and wanted to make a decision uninfluenced by her opinion. My mother has fantastic taste. She has mastered the art of dressing well, and is able to give fantastic fashion advice to accentuate the features and flaws of any body type. I don't know why I would have told her I didn't need her help, other than to assert my independence.

I had my boyfriend wear a coordinating cummerbund, bow tie and corsage ribbon. I made my last payment the Friday before the Prom in May, and excitedly carried a plastic wrapped dress out to my car with the shoes and purse. As soon as I got home, I slipped the shoes on my feet and attempted to zip up the back of the dress. I called my mom into help and turned to look at myself in my mirrored closet doors. My mother's eyes met mine in the mirror, and I couldn't contain the tears any longer.

I felt fat and ugly.

I had spent several hundred dollars to feel spectacular... to sparkle. All I could think, as I viewed my blurred image while sobbing, is that I looked like a reverse

Smurfette. I had a bright blue dress and pasty white skin versus her blue skin and white dress. Every sequin seemed to accentuate rolls and curves I wanted to mask. The dress was too short, too tight, and too low cut. It was not how I envisioned feeling for my Junior prom.

My mom just hugged me, and let me cry for a while before calmly asking what she could do to help. I explained through ragged sobs that there were no refunds or exchanges on special orders and lay-a ways at the bridal shop where I purchased the aqua blue sequined dress. I don't remember exactly how much it cost, I think around $300. It's a lot of money now, but in 1994, working part time making $5.20/ hr, it took over 2 months to pay for my outfit. My mom called the store, and was able to speak to the manager. She drove with me to exchange the dress for a simple little black dress I wore to another dance, but they kept the difference in cost. My friend lent me a sassy black dress to wear for the dance that night.

I was reminded of the aqua blue sequin dress today, and questioned why I bought it if it made me feel so physically uncomfortable and self conscious.

I listened to someone else and their opinion, instead of my inner voice.

A salesperson gushed about how gorgeous I looked, when I tried it on. Even though I could hear my inner voice question what she said, I ignored it. I wanted to believe her, and it was easier than admitting that something else would look more flattering on me.

Most of us spend high school and our early 20's defining who we are, and how we can sparkle best. We try out different clothing and hairstyles. We test different groups of friends, make-out buddies, college majors and jobs. We are searching for our perfect fit in life that accentuates our best attributes and minimizes our flaws.

With all of the noise of the world, it can be difficult at times to hear your inner voice.

I'm long past those teens and twenties, yet still find myself questioning at times how I fit in. We compare our lives, and bodies. We listen to the advice of strangers, instead of that inner voice. Sometimes, in our desire to stand out, we forget that we are enough as we are without all the flash... unless you are one of the few who can rock sequins. If you are an aqua blue sequin person though, let us see you sparkle.

Questions for Reflection

Take a moment to listen to your inner voice. What is it telling you?

Who we were

The foundation of who we were is important to reflect on when we consider who we want to become.

It's been 20 years since I graduated from high school. I am friends with most of my former classmates on Facebook. I know about their careers and families. I know about major changes that have occurred in their lives. I've witnessed their death of a parent, birth of a child, marriage, divorce, rehab, promotions, coming out of the closet, cancer. I know who has hair and who doesn't anymore. I know who is in better physical shape now, than 20 years ago, and who isn't.

My husband, and many of my classmates, probably don't see the point in buying a plane ticket to their hometown for a reunion. What's the point of spending time, money and an evening with people that they can message if they want to, but usually don't? Some people won't go, because they feel frustrated that 20 years later, they are not where they want to be in life, and that their path in life is set.

Others might have painful high school memories of bullying, betrayal and loneliness that they've spent the past 2 decades avoiding or resolving. I care about my former classmates not just for who they are or were, but for how our lives are permanently intertwined through shared experiences.

I am going to my 20 year high school reunion so that I can feel connected, and remind my classmates of who they were and who we have become.

Here are just a few things that I learned from my friends:

Too much of a good thing, is never a good thing.... especially when it involves raspberry liquor and Denny's grilled cheese sandwich.

Sometimes, the idea of an experience is better than the reality of it, especially if it has been built up to be magical, but it's not. Junior year prom picture, my eyes were closed, the room was really hot, and even though I arrived with someone I loved, I wished that I had the courage to slow dance with you instead.

I admire your tenacity. I saw where you started. I have pride in your accomplishments as you have become a teacher or physician, or triathlete, or entrepreneur or parent.

I've realized that what you valued 20 years ago, for the most part, you still do. I see it in your ambition to be the best in your field, the time you take to connect with friends and family, the way that you physically mark yourself as different to stand out from the crowd, the way that you seek out and connect with friends, and the time you've spent completing your degree online.

Thank you for getting in the drivers ed car when it was my turn.

Thanks for keeping my secrets... even when I told your parents yours.

I know it's been a long time, but I miss you.

Even though you didn't think I noticed you watching me in math class, I did... and looked forward to the attention every day.

Please, come to our reunion.

I want to see you without a photo filter. To tug your curly hair like I did during English class, and know the real stuff that a status update with well-groomed children doesn't reflect.

I want you to confide in me the way that you did when you told me about your parents and the pain you felt of not being able to measure up to their expectations. I want to hear you tell another self-deprecating joke that makes me laugh and remember all the other times you made us laugh at the lunch table, even though you carried so much pain with you.

I want to look at you, and remember.

I want to remember the shared experiences of state champion football games, homecoming dances, and plays. I want to remember DECA, drama, and Sophomore year scandals. I want to see how you have evolved and become greater than you imagined, and the ways that you wished that you were different.

Most importantly, I want you to see me for who I am now, while remembering who I was.

I want you to remind me that I can be dramatic, confident, funny, passionate and brave. I want you to remind me of the hope I had in myself and in my future, before years eroded my optimism.

I want you to look at me and remember shared intimacy that defined us, as we worked to become closer to who we are now.

I want you to know that our shared experiences are what I remember most about you. I want you to know that my hope for my children is to have the same defining impact on others that you have had and continue to have on me.

I'll see you soon.

Questions for reflection

How did your experiences in high school shape who you are today?

_____

_____

_____

_____

Have you attended a reunion with your high school classmates?

_____

_____

_____

Why or why not?

_____

_____

When you thought you could

We can not control what happens in our lives.
*We **can** control how we view our situation.*

Go back awhile, into those parts of your memory that you push aside. Remember with me. Do you remember when you thought you could? Do you remember how it felt... to believe? In yourself? Your abilities? Do you remember how it felt before someone convinced you that you couldn't? You believed in your greatness once. You were capable, and you knew it. It was part of your identity, crafted over time with positive reinforcement and validation.

You knew that you could, because you did. You had talent that your peers didn't, and you used it to grow, improve and become even greater. Your supporters told you, *you can do it..* and you did. What happened to change that? Was it an overnight epiphany, or an evolution of obstacles... obstacles that became too great in your mind to conquer? Barriers that you focused on rather than your ability, and talent and gift, and the overwhelming evidence otherwise.

At some point, you let the limitations and labels they placed on you define you.

Maybe it was a parent, or teacher, or coach. Maybe it was a boss, lover or friend. You listened to them more than your inner voice, and believed their lie. You swallowed the doubt until it was absorbed into the fiber of your gut.

Somehow, what they said, or the way they said it, or the fact that they were an Expert meant that they had credibility in a way you never gave yourself.

And the lie grew, because lies feed on failure and doubt, you know? They need to be hidden deep within, unexposed to truth, to fester. They are covered with shame. Lies are left to contaminate everything healthy around them. Lies grow if you don't root them out. Once you welcome the lies, they take over like a Biblical plague of locusts. The lies you tell yourself feed on your hopes and dreams. They leave a ravaged psyche behind. You're picked clean of life after the cloud descends. Barren of hope. And the worst thing is... it's preventable.

You swallowed their lie, and it became your truth.

So you hear...

You can't.

You're not.

You won't.

There's no way.

You don't deserve it.

And you listen to those lies in your mind because they must be right.

Maybe you've been repeating the lie for years, or decades, or even longer. The longer that you've eaten the lies which have become your truth, the harder it becomes to change. It becomes more difficult to shift your fixed mindset to believe that you can.

Do you remember when you thought you could?

I want you to question those lies. Discard the fear preventing your progress. Believe again. Believe that *you can*, that *you will*, that *it's possible*. I want you to cut out the cancer of doubt. Silence the whisper of shame. And if it's been there a long time, it may be painful. It may take time, diligence, and professional help to remove those lies from your mind. There's no shortcut to numb the process, to rip it away.... But *you must*.

Because, when you think you can, anything is possible.

Questions for reflection

What are the 3 biggest lies you've told yourself?

_____

_____

_____

_____

How would your life change if you no longer believed those lies?

_____

_____

_____

_____

Write positive affirmations to replace the lies. For example one of the lies I believed for years was "I am fat." I replaced that with the affirmation "My body is strong and healthy."

Our labels

The words we choose to describe ourselves and others matter.

I wore the white cotton mu-mu with orange hyacinth flowers along the bottom. I stuffed 3 small pillows and a teddy bear to create a round midsection cinched a waistline with an apron tied below the enormous bulge. I wore slippers. I donned a clear, plastic hotel shower cap, and carried a toy wooden rolling pin in one hand, to hit my husband on the head if he got out of line. I was a housewife for Halloween.

At 9, I can only guess how I formed this image of a housewife. I never witnessed someone hit with a rolling pin in real life. I recall Tom and Jerry cartoons with a woman who would chase after the animals with a rolling pin. My single mother had always worked full time in white collar office jobs 45 minutes away to support my brother and me. She drove us 20 minutes away to a better school district every morning before continuing her journey to work.

We lived in a rural, low-income, government subsidized housing development, and I had overheard my mother complaining about some of our neighbors. Her greatest frustrations were overweight housewives who collected government welfare checks, food stamps, smoked too many cigarettes, and stayed at home watching soap operas. Most of the neighborhood kids were unsupervised juvenile delinquents. (This probably seems like a gross exaggeration, but it isn't.)

I wore my costume to an overnight lock-in at the mall for my Girl Scout troop . It may have been our leader, or one of the other mothers with us who brought it to my attention. They were all housewives, but I never considered how they were different than most of the women in my neighborhood 20 minutes away.

I didn't realize my costume would offend them, but it did. As requested, I removed the shower cap, tucked away the rolling pin and slippers and was just a "fat lady". I don't think that was much better. (Ironically, I have always struggled with my weight.)

Calling myself a full-time homemaker, or housewife still makes my skin crawl a bit, though I've had years to adapt to my role. Our culture does not value full time caretakers and nurtures. Changing my job title to stay-at-home mom does little to improve the public's general perception of my role as a mother, wife and woman.

I taught a lesson for our women's organization, and loved this quote I found,

"We need to take a term which is sometimes spoken of with derision and elevate it. It is the term homemaker. All of us- women, men, youth and children, single or married – can work at being homemakers." -Bonnie L. Oscarson

I have performed varied tasks in my role as a full time homemaker over the past 8+ years including opening a small business with my husband. I know what I do as a homemaker has value. My role as a primary caregiver is a conscious decision my husband and I have made together for the long term benefit of our four sons. Yet, I still have difficulty reconciling how what I do defines who I am.

I was completing an application. There was a box that asked for my occupation. I left it blank. I was overwhelmed with the options of how to fill the box. Though it was how I spent most of my time, I was embarrassed to type Homemaker. I didn't want to be perceived as uneducated, and more importantly, insignificant.

An occupation can not fully measure the sum of an individual or who they are as a human being.

I want to be acknowledged for the contribution I make. It is how I have shaped my identity, and my perceived value as a person. I know that I am not alone.

The girls I attended middle school and high school with have accomplished phenomenal things in their careers as women. Some do not have children, some balance demanding careers with motherhood, and others have left or adapted careers to be full time homemakers.

I am grateful for the opportunity our generations of women have to choose how to focus their time and energy. I think it is especially difficult for these brilliant women who have chosen to become full time homemakers/ full time caregivers for their children.

A part of me bristles when they are viewed as a "homemaker" rather than a corporate attorney with a Harvard Law degree, or as a mom who sews, rather than a Botanist and scientific researcher. They are defined as the woman who knits hats for her kids instead of a Non-profit founder, grant writer and Community Activist. They become the women's church group leader instead of a news anchor, journalist and college professor. Their labels minimize both the importance of the work they are doing, as well as the contributions they had in careers before becoming mothers.

These women, and many others aren't less intelligent or accomplished due to decisions they have made to devote their time and attention to homemaking and child-rearing.

I would argue that these homemakers struggle to become more through sacrifice, and delaying or shifting personal career goals to nurture and support the needs of their families. It has been difficult for me to balance the needs of my family with nurturing my mind, passions and personal development.

My mind hungers for constant intellectual stimulation. When you devote your time to a goal that isn't easily quantifiable except by redundant tasks like neatly folded laundry and mopped floors, it can be easy to dismiss the value, contribution, or intellectual aptitude of a full time homemaker.

This is something we can work together to change.

Jen's Challenge

I challenge you to ask the next time you meet someone new to ask them about what they are passionate about, rather than their occupation. This can be especially important when you interact with a full-time homemaker, or someone who is unemployed or retired. Although it is more common for someone identifying as female to be the primary caregiver for children, or homemaker, that has shifted in the past decade as "traditional" household roles are being reevaluated.

The next time you meet a new person, ask them about how they nurture their mind.

Ask a stranger how they find joy and accomplishment in life.

Listen.

I have realized when you ask questions like these, rather than "what they do" people are more vulnerable and honest. It creates an opportunity for deep and authentic connection with others. People ask questions like that so rarely.

Asking these questions can put people at ease if they are unemployed, especially if it was not by choice like so many people right now. It may give you insight about creating more meaning in your life. It also might help you value housewives, stay at home parents, and full-time homemakers more.

The foundation of our support system

We all need people who know, understand and appreciate the authentic us.

My 20 year high school reunion was epic. It was epic, because after years of searching for who I am and where I fit in, *I belonged*. I was home. I was surrounded by friends, and acceptance.

I hesitated before typing the word on Facebook to describe my 20 year high school reunion. I said, "It was epic". As expected, another former classmate, who lives out of state, and was unable to attend the reunion called me on it.

"Define epic?"

It wasn't *epic* like a summer blockbuster movie. There wasn't a brawl between a former jock and an outcast like a distant relative's 20 year reunion. (Thankfully). It was *epic* like Homer's Odyssey. It was like the hero's defining moment when he realizes he already possessed the trait's he'd been searching for on his quest.

It was life affirming.

Spending an evening with people I went to high school with, reminded me of what I liked most about them. It reminded me of why I, for the most part, enjoyed high school. I was able to spend time with people who have logged more hours with me and witnessed a lot of my character defining moments. Newer friends won't have that same experience. My family members are the only other people in my life that will do that. Because we are related, their perspectives may tint our perception of the same situation.

I spent my reunion talking, laughing, taking pictures, and smiling. I smiled so much, that my cheeks hurt after 3 hours ...and it felt great. It was epic, because after years of searching for who I am and where I fit in, *I belonged.* I was home. I was surrounded by friends, and acceptance.

I didn't have to waste time making small talk to feel a person out, because I already had established relationships. I was able to bypass the getting-to-know-you pleasantries and dive into the deep stuff I cared about. I was able to just be Jen... without all of the labels, and burdens I carry with me most of the time. I felt a sense of peace and belonging in a way that I haven't in a long time. I was home.

As an adult, it can be difficult to make new friends.

Friends are often chosen by circumstances like where you live or work, or children with similar ages or your church attendance. With adult responsibilities, time spent with friends can fall to the bottom of the list of priorities. Relationships take time and energy to nurture, and we have a finite supply of both. I haven't made it a very high priority, and now realize that I need to spend more time with friends. I would encourage you to do the same if it's been awhile.

My 20 year high school reunion was epic, because I realized that over the past year preparing for the reunion, and past 2 decades searching for who I am, plenty of people know and like me. Sometimes, it takes spending time with people who have known you for a long time to remember who you are.

Questions for reflection

Do you find it difficult to show others your authentic self? Why?

_____

_____

_____

_____

Who in your life knows the "real you" best? Why?

_____

_____

_____

_____

How I fixed the dresser I should have said no to

Broken things and broken people can be mended.

I had been looking for a new dresser for over a year. I've spent enough time on Pinterest exploring links to dresser make-overs to know that I wanted something made out of solid wood and not laminate. It is hard to find well constructed furniture. Most is flat packed to put together with allen wrenches. I like solid.

I like furniture with a story.

When I saw pictures of 2 dressers pop up on part of a local Buy Sell Trade Facebook page I was excited. The seller wanted $30 each for them. I thought they looked like solid wood. I committed to buy them, and she offered to deliver them to my place for an extra $20 so I wouldn't have to load the boys in the van for a 40 minute car ride. Plus, with 4 boys in the van, where would I put the dressers? We settled on $10 for delivery. She said that she would be by Sunday morning. I was in a hurry to leave for church the next day when she stopped by with her husband to drop off the dressers. Both dressers were damaged in the transport. They were scratched, and the flimsy board attached to the back was bent. the plastic holding it was bent out of shape, cracked and falling off.

There were crayon scribbles on one dresser that hadn't been visible in the picture online. The dresser was laminate on the sides and interior drawers. When she said she felt bad and her husband had damaged them moving them, and didn't know if I would still want them, I wasn't honest. I said it wasn't a problem... even though it was. I had never met this woman before. She had given me an out. I didn't really have $70 in the first place to spend on dressers, especially if they were broken. There was no way that they would hold up to 4 boys banging drawers shut, or shoving jeans in them. I gave her the money, thanked her, and she left.

And I cried.... hot angry tears for not standing up for myself. For not being honest and saying, "Look lady, I would maybe give you $10 for this dresser the way it is now." I cried, because

I was polite instead of being honest.

The next day, I started sanding the wood on top. The drawers I hoped were sturdy and looked like real wood were particle boards and laminate. I removed the hardware from the drawers and I cried some more. After I removed the broken backing, the dresser was flimsy, and I didn't know what I would do to fix it.

I couldn't sand the scrapes out of the sides. I let it sit in the garage for a month. Every time I opened the garage door, it reminded me of my inability to stand my ground, and my stomach churned.

With the seasons changing, I needed more space for my boys clothes, and found another dresser. I refinished it, and it turned out beautifully. I revisited the broken dresser with confidence it could be fixed.

I palm sanded the drawers and top. I used my favorite shade of blue paint in a wash and added 2 coats to each drawer face.

I grabbed pallet wood from my garage and mounted it with 1 5/8″ hunter green deck screws.

I added my signature mismatched hardware to give it an eclectic look. Plus, I have a stash of sample drawer pulls I've been hoarding that I bought for only $1 each when the nearby hardware store changed owners.

After adding the interior wood strip and new back, the dresser is stronger. It will be able to handle more. I could have donated the broken down dresser, or taken it to the dump as I contemplated after lots of tears. I persevered and reinforced the structure instead. I can't wait to put it to use.

Sometimes, all it takes is looking at something differently to realize that you don't have a hot mess in front of you... you have something with possibilities and lots of potential.

The Scream

Listen to the whisper of your spirit

I don't remember the first time I saw the painting in my teenage years, but I do remember how I felt... disturbed. I also questioned the artist Edvard Munch's mental state at the time he painted it. There were heavy brush strokes like Vincent Van Gough's paintings, and I had already learned that Van Gough cut off his ear. Then, he proceeded to paint a self portrait showing off his bandaged head... not exactly the epitome of mental stability. I haven't spent time studying images of The Scream for years, but it disturbs me as an adult in a way that it didn't as a teenager.

There have been times I have felt like the androgynous, bald figure screaming in the foreground of that painting. There are anxious lines of worry, distress, and probable lack of sleep, rimming the eyes. The person appears isolated though there are 2 figures in the background. It makes me wonder...

Why paint a scream if no one can hear it?
More importantly, Why am I screaming?

I've spent a lot of time revisiting the second question the past 3 years. I want to be heard, but the ironic thing is that screaming isn't usually the best way to go about it. People who scream too often, are the boy who cried wolf, or chicken little with a falling sky.

Screamers are over-exaggerating political commentators. They are social media, soapbox-ranting vigilanties. They are usually ignored... regardless of what they are screaming about. With all of the noise in our world today, it can be the whisper that is more readily heard than the scream.

It can be the whispered confidence of a spouse or friend. It can be the whispered prayers for strength to endure a trial. It can be the whispering of your soul to make a life change. It may be the whispering of the wind around you as you search for peace in nature. When I am screaming to voice my frustrations about the path I am on in life, or how it isn't what I planned or envisioned for myself, I miss the whispers.

Maybe, the person in the painting is not really screaming on the outside, but on the inside, waiting for someone to listen, and help. Our minds are so important to us, and we use them to judge danger in a situation. We analyze the world around us, and our place in it. What happens when your brain lies to you though? What happens when you are the dehumanized figure in the painting, screaming for help, but no one around you is alarmed?

Is your brain lying to you, or is there a problem you don't know how to articulate any other way, except through a scream?

Questions for reflection

Do you feel like screaming lately?

_____

_____

_____

Have you figured out why?

_____

_____

_____

What action can you take to quiet your inner screams, and hear your inner voice more clearly?

_____

_____

_____

5 tips for setting goals

Reaching a goal is even better than setting one.

I love setting goals for myself. Most people wait for the beginning of the calendar year to set a goal. Often in two weeks or later, those goals are abandoned. A transition time in life is the perfect time to set personal goals.

Here are my 5 best tips to reach the goals you set.

5. Don't just think it, ink it.

Write your goal down. It can be on a note card you tape to the bathroom mirror, tape to your dashboard in the car or in your wallet. You will be more likely to reach your goal with that visual reminder.

4. Set a realistic goal.

One New Year, I had 3 note cards full of goals. One card for the body, one for the mind, and one for spirit. I reached a couple of the goals I had on my cards over the course of the year, but still felt like a failure when I looked at everything I didn't accomplish. If you reach your goal before the end of the year, wonderful! Then, you can set more. Pace yourself, so you don't quit because you feel overwhelmed. You don't need 500 subdivided goals. Pick 1 or 2.

3. *Create goal mileposts.*

After I set my goals to lose 100 lbs and complete my first triathlon, I made sure that I had mileposts to check in along my journey to the goals I set. With my weight loss, it was pound increments in addition to larger mile posts like shopping for new pants in a "regular" store or department not geared toward plus sized women.

2. *Clear your personal roadblocks.*

I don't like to exercise. I love how I feel when I'm done, but the process isn't fun to me. Knowing this, I have to trick myself into doing it. I prepare my clothes the night before to create a smoother morning routine. I have used a workout buddy that I know will be waiting for me to get out of the house. My favorite trick, that I am using now, is to give myself gold stars. I have Post-it stars that I mark the date and exercise I do, and stick them on the mirror.

It is a great way for me to see my progress over time. Plus, I am rewarding myself with a couple new digital music downloads for my workout when I reach 100 stars.

1. *Be Persistent.*

It can be challenging overcoming an addiction or forming a positive habit. (I've acquired and given up many bad habits over the years. True story.) If you're at all like me, you will have days where you want to quit trying, and you may lose focus dealing with day to day challenges. You might temporarily relapse into old patterns. What separates the goal setters from the goal achievers is the doing. It is also the ability to fall or make a mistake, and keep going.

Jen's Challenge

Set a goal. You can use a classic index card, in addition to writing it here. Heck, you can hang it on every mirror in your house, the car, and on your refrigerator. Just make sure you can see it often to remind you. *Bonus Points-* Share your goal. More people can lead to greater goal accountability. (Unless your goal is to run a marathon. I read a study that it actually makes it less likely to run one the more people you tell about your goal to run one.)

What's the biggest goal you've ever achieved? (It doesn't matter how long ago it was.)

_____

_____

_____

What was your original motivation for setting it?

_____

_____

_____

_____

What/who helped you reach your goal?

_____

_____

_____

What did you do to celebrate accomplishing the goal?

_____

_____

_____

My new goal is...

_____

_____

_____

Day one

The starting part is only part of change.

As a habitual quitter, you know that it's not day one that's hard. It's the next day, and the day after, and the rest of the days that you are trying to change. You know, because you have had a lot of day ones.

On day one, you are determined, and motivated to become better. You are capable of more, and you are going to prove that this time it is different than your other failed attempts. This time, you have learned. This time, you will avoid your usual triggers.

This time, you are granite.

This time...

The other times you failed do not matter. You were preparing for *this* day one. You know that it will take time to see results, and you are committed to your goal. You are strong. You will hush the critic in your mind with action.

Today is the last day one.

You just need to make it through the next day, and the day after that, and the day after that.

Questions for reflection

What motivates you?

_____

_____

What 3 things have derailed you from reaching goals you've set for yourself in the past or sticking with something?

_____

_____

_____

What will you do to proactively prevent goal derailment this time? Make a plan.

_____

_____

_____

Our Perception

Your life experiences shape the way you see the world.

"Wow. That's a lot of junk food you've got there."

I turned and smiled at the guy behind me in line eyeing the contents of my grocery cart as I set items on the conveyor belt to check out. "Yes it is, but it's New Year's Eve. It's a night to splurge."

"Well, that's still an awful lot of chips for you to eat."

I heard the implication in his tone of voice and saw it in his facial expression. *You shouldn't be eating that. Why aren't you on a diet?*

I was being fat shamed.

Shamed by a stranger at the grocery store. Two hours ago, I was feeling fantastic about the way I looked today. I felt like I was channeling Audrey Hepburn from Sabrina. I was wearing my vintage plum wool coat, black turtleneck and red lipstick. I was wearing pants that hadn't fit in over a year. I had felt so great this morning, I took a selfie and updated my Facebook profile. I placed the last bottle of sparkling cider on the conveyor belt. I turned, made direct eye contact with him, and plastered my best smile I cultivated during 15+ years of customer service work.

"Well, it's a good thing that I've lost 13 pounds already during the holidays with all of the running I've been doing. I can eat as much of this as I want, and I'm not going to feel guilty about it at all."

"Huh…. How'd ya manage to lose weight during the holidays?"

"I have will power."

In the past, I would have felt the need to explain or justify my grocery cart contents. I might have told this self-appointed food police officer that I have 4 boys at home that will eat most of the chips over the course of the next 2 weeks in their school lunches.

I would have mentioned we usually only grocery shop once every two weeks, or less for the six of us. I would have pointed out that the chips were buy one, get one free.

I would have said we were dipping our Keebler cookies in chocolate fondue, because I was too exhausted this year to whip up any cookies from scratch. I would have told him that this was the third store I'd been to in the last hour gathering ingredients for our special New Year's Eve family fondue dinner, and my car was full of produce for the organic salad with which we were beginning our feast.

I wanted to poke his protruding middle-aged belly with my finger out of spite, and make the Pillsbury doughboy giggle noise, or some other snarky remark about *his* body mass index.

But I didn't.

None of that matters.

If he had said, "Hey, can I come to your house for dinner? Those chips look great." I probably would have would have laughed. I may have even opened the bag and offered him a few after I paid for them.

But, he didn't say that to me.

Is a 5'4″ medium-sized lady really going to drink 6 bottles of sparkling cider, cherry 7-up, 3 bags of chips, 3 types of cookies, garlic bread, salami, Triscuits, jumbo marshmallows, a red and green bell pepper and a bottle of white balsamic vinegar by herself in one sitting? And, so what if I did?

Public shaming comes as a natural response too easily to most of us. It is a lot easier to point out differences or flaws than seek to show understanding for strangers.

Some people may not show outward signs of their trials or troubles. But we can show compassion, and give strangers the benefit of the doubt. Not everybody is a jerk.

Maybe, the guy behind me in line wasn't fat shaming me at all.

Spread compassion for strangers. Forgive someone you know... like a family member. Assume that a person wasn't *trying* to hurt you. Or maybe they did mean to hurt you, but you can fight back by choosing to let it go.

Forgiveness doesn't mean you have to spend time with a past abuser. Forgiving someone doesn't mean you have to accept what happened is okay. It doesn't mean you have to communicate with the person at all.

Letting go of the hurt someone caused you leaves more room for love and peace in your life. This could be the year that you choose peace.

Jen's Challenge

If you haven't seen the dramatization of David Foster Wallace's commencement speech, "This is Water", watch it. You can find it through a YouTube search. If you've already seen it, watch it again, because it's that good.

Questions for reflection

What clarity have you gained through this process?

_____

_____

_____

After completing the workbook reflection questions, it's time for *you* to define yourself. Look back through the exercises you've completed. What are your 3 best attributes / characteristics?

_____

_____

_____

See the good in you. What 3 words would you use to describe the authentic you?

_____

_____

_____

Congratulations! These 3 words are the foundation of your personal brand. They help others see the good in you and what you do.

A note from the author

Parting words

Personal Branding authentically requires knowing who you are, and being able to see the good in you and what you do.

It involves introspection, forgiveness, withholding judgement, listening to your inner voice and letting go of negative labels. It's cultivating a support system of people who embrace the authentic version of us. It's moving past shame, building our legacy, setting goals, and embracing our situation by shifting our perspective.

Finding clarity for your personal brand is an ongoing process.

Transition times may guide us to rebrand and redefine who we are. We can use our transition times to grow, learn, improve and change.

Or not.

It is always a choice.

What will you choose?

FAQs

How can I work with you, Jen?

As a Personal Branding Expert and Entrepreneurial Connector, I help people gain clarity to expand their community, connections, and conversions through strategy, coaching and mentorship. You can find more information about my services: https://www.redlipsmarketing.com/contact-me/

Is there a workbook bonus?

Heck yeah! https://www.redlipsmarketing.com/bonus/

What other resources do you offer ?

Subscribe to my mailing list, download printables, learn more about my workshops, webinars and speaking engagements, and second book:

I've got my 3 words. Now what?

When I work one on one with clients, I use their 3 words to guide in the fundamentals of creating a brand kit for them. It helps me with the process for everything from color choice, logo design, web design, marketing, headshot photos and market positioning.

I've realized when people don't have clarity around the key fundamentals of their personal brand, the physical elements of their marketing don't have the authenticity that people crave... especially if you're targeting Gen-Z who were born 1995 -2007.

What if I don't have 3 words yet?

That's okay. It may take time for you to define them. You can start the process of personal branding without them, it just might take a bit more work.

What if I have more than 3 words?

That's totally okay. It gives you more to work with as you market your personal brand.

Can I change my words?

Yes. Transition times, and therapy may shift both the way you see the good in you and what you do. Be kind to yourself. Your words can be aspirational, but should also reflect the authentic you... I would never choose the word calm for myself. If you've met me in person, you'd understand why.

How can I connect with you?

On LinkedIn: https://www.linkedin.com/in/jencampbellteaches/

On Instagram: https://www.instagram.com/jencampbellteaches/

On Facebook: https://www.facebook.com/JenCampbellTeaches

I would love to hear from you!

Made in the USA
Columbia, SC
20 November 2020

24965325R00041